Everything Is Your Fault

Understanding the 6 Pillars to Unlocking Your Bliss Life

BY LIA BLISS

B.

BlissPoint Press
San Jose, California

ISBN: 978-1-7368462-9-2 - Hardback
ISBN: 979-8-9863478-0-6 - Paperback
ISBN: 979-8-9863478-1-3 - eBook

Everything Is Your Fault : Understanding the 6 Pillars to Unlocking Your Bliss Life by Lia Bliss

Published by BlissPoint Press.

www.BlissPointPress.com.

9 781736 846292

Everything Is Your Fault

Understanding the 6 Pillars to Unlocking Your Bliss Life

In the words of Snoop Dogg:

I want to thank me for believing in me, I want to thank me for doing all this hard work. I wanna thank me for having no days off. I wanna thank me for never quitting. I wanna thank me for always being a giver and trying to give more than I receive. I wanna thank me for trying to do more right than wrong. I wanna thank me for being me at all times.

CONTENTS

part 1

EVERYTHING IS YOUR FAULT

No more excuses. No more blaming your current state on a long and well-kept list of "other" things that caused you to be in this circumstance.

There is only you.

Everything is your fault.

The first response to hearing this is generally a negative one. But be kind to yourself. Give yourself the grace you so desperately need and readily give to others.

Then begin to look at all the magical things you get to take credit for. You may not be proud of everything in your life, but you've done some pretty amazing things so far. Take credit for the good; that's your fault too.

Once you can begin to embrace that everything is your fault, you start to understand the power that you hold. Once you stop making excuses and start making changes, you'll see that you've always had the power.

Enter – Bliss Life.

What is Bliss Life?

First and foremost, Bliss Life is your fault, or it will be.

Bliss Life is the goal. It's the place you arrive when you've taken full responsibility for your life and taken advantage of your power. Bliss Life is the life you get to live when you are in perfect alignment with your highest and most powerful version of yourself.

Bliss Life is living on a farm, raising your family, and running your home decor empire – if you're Johanna Gains, that is.

Bliss Life is finding out you're secretly the heir to a small European country and still choosing the boy next door, quitting your toxic "dream job" in fashion editing even though you got the Gucci boots, or being Catwoman... I see you, Anne Hathaway.

Bliss Life is whatever you define it as, but most importantly, it's what ONLY YOU define it as. Attaining a Bliss Life comes with a strong sense of self-awareness.

A word of caution to this tale.

Better than bad is not good.

Let me restate; moving from a terrible situation to a slightly better one is not the goal. The goal is to live a Bliss Life. A life that has you weeping for joy at the mere thought of the reality you're in, an overwhelming sense of accomplishment, pride, and satisfaction in the life you have created.

Not just slightly better than wherever you are now. Do not settle for better-than-bad. You deserve a fabulous life filled with joy, grace, and ease.

You can't live the life of your dreams if you can't identify exactly what makes you happiest. Simple self-awareness makes all the difference.

Are you a night owl but were told you need a high-powered job that demands you be in the office at 6 am every day? Do you value freedom? Money? Travel opportunities? Job security? Knowing yourself is the first step towards living a life that lights you up, makes you feel alive, fills you with – dare I say, Bliss?

I love the definition of self-awareness as proposed by psychologists Shelley Duval and Robert Wicklund:

"Self-awareness is the ability to focus on yourself and how your actions, thoughts, or emotions do or don't align with your internal standards. If you're highly self-aware, you can objectively evaluate yourself, manage your emotions, align your behavior with your values, and correctly understand how others perceive you."

Developing self-awareness is important because it allows you to assess your growth and effectiveness and course-correct when necessary.

Alas, the path to your Bliss Life is not a neat and tidy yellow brick road. It's not even a well-worn path. It is the road less traveled, and because you are the only person defining your Bliss Life, there will be times when the way becomes uncertain. You'll need to draw yourself a map, and the map towards your Bliss Life is paved in goals.

How do you know what goals to set to start you on the path?

Start with identifying the feeling you want to have.

First, go listen to Jai Wolf — "It All Started With A Feeling."

I'll wait.

You are only going to be truly committed to your goals if you're committed on an emotional level.

We're not talking about what you want to accomplish or what you want to possess because the power of manifesting and the path to creating your Bliss Life starts with how you want to feel.

As you build your goals, the initial motivation can often be how you DON'T want to feel. The desire to change ourselves, our surroundings, and circumstances often comes from a catalyst moment. An "enough is enough" straw-that-broke-the-camel's-back moment.

This moment will vary from extreme to subtle depending on how close you are to your vision of your Bliss Life.

If your vision of your Bliss Life is different from the life you're living now, then there may be a desire to take drastic measures. Burn it all down and start over, move to a different city, reinvent ourselves, or — gasp — cut bangs.

Our instincts are to overhaul our lives, take extreme measures and start from scratch.

I will advise against this.

You may feel as though you are leagues away from where you want to be, and once you've decided to make the shift, it can be hard to be patient with the process.

But that's exactly what I'm going to ask you to do.

Subtle shifts to how you feel and how you identify yourself have further-reaching effects than short bursts of effort that inevitably put you right back where you started, only more discouraged.

Knowing what you want is the first step. It's the most important step. Resist the temptation to jump ahead to overambitious and unplanned actions; focus on the process.

Envisioning a Bliss Life, a life you're happy to wake up to every day, gives you a target to aim at, a direction to follow. Knowing specifically what you want provides clarity in decision-making. Remember your self-awareness and begin to see your goal in the distance.

The fastest way to identify your first steps towards your Bliss Life goal and get better acquainted with how you want to feel is to think back to a time when you felt the most successful.

What did your life look like then?
What were you doing or not doing?
How close were you to your Bliss Life?

Compare that time of your life to now.

What has shifted in your current state of being and feeling?
What elements of that time would you like to bring back?
What can you do right now to regain that feeling of success?

After answering these questions, you will be able to identify your Macro goal. A Macro goal is a large-scale goal, specifically the system that will help you achieve the feeling and life you desire.

No matter what you want to manifest new into your Bliss Life, consistency is the key.

Good habit forming, goal achieving, and arriving at your Bliss Life comes down to consistency. And here's the secret: Consistency is for lazy people.

When you've built habits and are consistent in working towards your goals, you have the luxury of thinking less because you've already made your mind up about the actions you'll take to get there.

Making a decision truly sets you free. The problem most people have is that they don't know how to decide. Most people are so afraid of failure that they build a loophole into their decision, and it's the most horrific word in the world.

TRY.

I'm going to *try* to lose weight, *try* to quit smoking, *try* to run a marathon, or *try* to save a percentage of my paychecks each month. But as a wise Jedi master once said,

"Do, or do not. There is no try."

If you don't believe me or haven't seen *Star Wars,* do this exercise. Draw yourself a nice hot bath: add all the lavender-scented bath bombs and expensive oils you've been saving, put your phone on airplane mode, and tell your family on pain of death they are not to disturb you!

Now *try* and get in the bath.

You'll quickly realize that you either did or did not get in the tub. There is no *try*. You either enjoyed a relaxing soak, or you didn't, wasting all that expensive bath oil.

CHOOSE YOUR NEW IDENTITY

When it comes to setting your goals, you must make up your mind with absolute certainty, "This is what I want."

Do you really want to have a Bliss Life? Then commit to doing whatever it takes.

DECIDE how you want to feel. DECIDE to change your life, your circumstances, your waistline, or the number in your bank account. If you're not committed to the change, why "try?" Why go through the motions half-heartedly?

Why play charades, pretending you're changing and striving for a Bliss Life, all the while not truly taking responsibility for yourself and your goal?

Save yourself the headache and don't read the rest of this book until you have DECIDED, with unfailing certainty, that you are going to go after that Bliss Life.

Deciding is the hardest part, but once you've decided, the rest of your choices become easier. You're not going to have to decide moment by moment if you're going to stick to the plans you've made. You've already made up your mind.

After you've planted yourself firmly in your decision, now comes the fun part. You get to start laying the foundation for the habits and routines that will shape your Bliss Life.

Because creating your Bliss Life isn't about the finish line.

The changes that new and exciting goals will bring to your life have very, very little to do with a single accomplishment. This is important to remember when picking your goals.

"How do I want to feel?" is the first question. The second is, "Who do I want to be?"

If one of the goals on your path to your Bliss Life is to run in the Boston Marathon or swim the English Channel, you probably started with the desire to feel proud and accomplished. However, you will never do great things unless you truly believe that you are the type of person who does them.

What does that mean? The first step to running the Boston marathon is to begin to identify as a "runner."

Equally, swimming the English Channel is only accomplished by "swimmers."

Before you lace up your sneakers or take that first jump into the lap pool, you've got to identify yourself as the type of person who accomplishes the goal you are setting out to achieve.

If my goal were, "I want to have calm and intentional mornings that make me feel energized, motivated, and excited for the day ahead. I want to avoid feeling rushed, anxious, and late every day." I'd need to ask myself the following questions:

What type of person has calm and intentional mornings?

Who is the person who wakes up motivated and energized?

I suggest that this person must have strong, consistent morning AND evening routines.

They are the type of person who doesn't hit snooze but hits the hay early enough to get plenty of sleep.

This person isn't running around because they forgot they have an early meeting, don't know what to wear, and can't find their keys.

No, this type of person that accomplishes the goals they're aiming for has an evening and morning routine that supports them.

This mindset is true of anyone who has accomplished BIG goals in their life.

Remember, once you've decided that nothing can knock you off your path toward your goal, and you've paved the way to achieve it, it will take effort to NOT get to that Bliss Life.

For example, if you've identified that you're the type of person who always puts 15% of their paycheck immediately into savings, you've set up automatic payments every two weeks into that savings account. It will take more work, more hassle, to un-save that money. The lazy thing to do would be to let the money keep being deposited into savings.

For myself, I identify as someone who eats healthy. I've laid the foundation by using a healthy meal kit delivery service and getting my family addicted to morning smoothies. It would take so much work to eat donuts for breakfast. I'd have to drive to the store, get the donuts, pay for them, and bring them home. The lazy option is to let the delivery service send smoothie ingredients every week.

In essence, don't rely on your motivation. Your new identity will feel abnormal at first – you'll be tempted to fall back into old habits. Create an environment that supports you.

And so, to begin this process for yourself, start with the most important questions. Answer them truthfully.

Remember, this is YOUR Bliss Life, not your mother, partner, or someone on Instagram telling you what your life should be like. But you, getting courageously honest about what you want.

"How do I want to feel?" "Who do I want to be?"

The answers to these questions should be broad and general.

For example:

I want to feel healthy.

I want to be someone who is in great shape.

I want to feel calm and intentional.

I want to be someone who has a consistent morning and evening routine and who's always ready for the day ahead.

I want to feel financially secure.

I want to be someone who manages their money well.

The next step in figuring out your goals is to identify what that person (who will soon be you) actually does. This is where you get incredibly specific about your goals.

Traditional rules of goal setting say that your goals must be SMART.

Specific
Measurable
Attainable
Realistic
Timely

Get specific, figure out how to measure your progress, keep them within reasonable limits and set a date to aim for.

Now, this is a lovely acronym, but like I've said, living a Bliss Life is not about getting to the finish line, although that can be a great motivator.

I'd like to suggest a different list. Take your goals through this checklist as each element will build upon the next:

Emotional — How you want to feel.

Personal — Who you want to be, how do you define the feeling of who you want to be.

Literal — What you're specifically going to do.

Measurable — How you track your progress.

Sustainable — Something that will stay with you long-term.

Yes, EPLMS isn't as catchy as SMART, but we're not talking about losing 30 pounds and then reverting to old eating habits or saving ten thousand dollars just to blow it on impulse purchases.

YOUR WINNING STRATEGY

Failure to plan is a plan to fail. You can say that you will work out every day, always be prepared for the day ahead, and start saving more. But unless you have a plan in place, you'll fall right back into old habits.

Back to our example — we want to feel calm, energized, and motivated every day. We are becoming the type of person with strong morning and evening routines and is always cool, calm, and collected no matter what comes our way.

But what do these routines look like?

Here's where reverse engineering comes in. Reverse engineering is a great way to build a plan for any goal. Start by getting very clear about how you want the result to look, then work backward, filling in the gaps.

Your goal is to get to work each morning feeling calm, motivated, and energized.

That means you didn't stress about traffic because you left the house with plenty of time to get to work.

You left the house early because you weren't hunting for lost keys or trying on every outfit, possibly after hitting the snooze button five times.

You found everything you needed because you set them out the night before. Outfit chosen, keys by the door, coffee maker full and timer ready to go, all done before you brushed your teeth and went to bed at a reasonable hour.

Your routine basically created itself through the process of reverse engineering.

So, what happens when your friends tell you about this sweet underground spot with an amazing band playing and "you have GOT to get down here right now?"

I'm not going to tell you to become a hermit, chained to your routines. But, if you've got "an amazing opportunity" to neglect your routines every other night, it seems like someone hasn't truly decided to commit to how they want to feel and who they want to be.

The old you went out at every suggestion of a night drinking with friends, but "if you always do what you've always done, you'll always get what you've always got," as they say.

Stay dedicated to the you **you** want to be. Stay dedicated to achieving your Bliss Life, but don't forget to live life along the way. This is where self-awareness will come heavily into play. Remember how everything is your fault? Yes. That also means that you get to make decisions because you're always in charge.

Check-in with yourself: do you *really* want to do this thing or participate in this opportunity?

Ask yourself these questions:
Will this thing bring me closer to my goals?
Will this thing take me further from my goals?

And then use your judgment; you have breathing room, you can wiggle, you are in control.

There's the saying "scared money doesn't make money," but it applies to every aspect of our lives as well. Scared action doesn't lead to opportunities. Be brave. See your goal in the distance but don't get hung up on planning exactly how you're going to get there.

In addition, do not try and overhaul your entire life in one week (Looking at you "New Year New Me").

Start slowly, stay consistent, look for opportunities that will take you in the right direction even if the path ahead isn't clear.

Once you've gotten the basics down and know the general direction you're headed, you can begin to add complexity to your life and goals.

MANIFESTING YOUR DREAMS

Everything is your fault. But that doesn't mean there aren't things outside of your control.

We can control our environment, reactions, routines, and our attitudes and as we build our Bliss Life, we focus on the things that we can adapt, shift, and change to suit the lives we're creating.

And yet, try as we might, we can't control everything.

We can't convince our dream job to accept us on the first application. We can't force the cutie at the coffee shop to fall madly in love with us at first sight and whisk us away to a fairy tale romance.

This is where Manifestation comes into play.

One of my favorite passages from *Where the Red Fern Grows* (keep tissues handy) is where the young man has spent all night trying to chop down a tree; he's done everything within his control to get the tree to fall. Finally, he offers up a prayer and asks God to handle the rest, and BOOM down comes the tree.

While I'm not a religious person, this example outlines the basics of Manifestation. Do all you can; leave the rest up to a Higher Power.
I'll be using the term "the Universe" in this book, but it can denote any form of Higher Power or Powers.

In my extensive work with Manifestation, I've identified the two different Manifestation styles:

The first is Specific Manifesting. I have a friend who calls it "Placing your order with the Universe."

As you can imagine, this type of Manifestation involves getting very specific with what you want.

Think of your universal request as your Starbucks order: Grande sugar-free vanilla latte with almond milk, an extra shot of espresso, and one pump of toffee syrup.

Tell the Universe, down to the letter, what you want, and don't settle for ANYTHING less.

The second type of Manifestation I like to think of as Co-creation Manifesting. This method involves a lot more focus on how you want to feel, and unlike Specific Manifesting, it allows the Universe to fill in all the blanks.

I used this Manifesting technique when building my dream job. I knew I wanted to work from home. I knew I wanted to have creative freedom, teach people, and make a lot of money without working a lot of hours. But the specifics of what exactly I'd be doing day by day, I left to the Universe.

Our ability to see our highest potential is often limited by our own scope of imagination.

I could never have imagined all the specific aspects of the work I do today. I left those details in the hands of the Universe and followed the path that kept me most aligned with how I wanted to feel.

For you, I suggest a hybrid approach to manifesting to add another layer of magic and intention.

No matter your goals, you can use a combination of these manifesting techniques to achieve your Bliss Life.

For example, if your goal is to experience more romance in your life — whether with a specific significant other or as an independent agent looking for love —you can use these techniques to achieve the romantic life you're after.

Start with Specific Manifesting. Identify the things that you know that you want in that romantic life. Do you want weekly date nights? A partner whose love language is Gifts or Words of Affirmation? Get crazy clear on what you want.

For me, I knew I wanted someone who was marriage-minded, someone who was on board with going after a Bliss Life, and someone who could push me to grow and become more.

I put in an order with the Universe.

Next, incorporate Co-creative Manifesting. Decide on the concepts or feelings you want to have: love, romance, a feeling of deep emotional support, a dedicated monogamous partner, etc. But release control of the specifics, like how tall they are or when and where you'll meet them, to the universe.

Essentially, know which things are an absolute must and leave room for the Universe to fill in the spaces with things you could never have imagined. My mom refers to this as a MUST-HAVE list and a WOULD-BE-NICE list. Even though her categorization is helpful, it's a little oversimplified, but you get the idea.

Very important: Commit to the Universe that you won't settle for less than what you want. Then, you can start breaking down the steps. This is where you take aligned action.

part 2

LET SELF-AWARENESS BE YOUR GUIDE

Start showing up to your Bliss Life.

The 6 Pillars, and truly the six relationships that make up your Bliss Life are:

1. Self
2. Higher Power
3. Tribe
4. Network
5. Money
6. Time

In Bliss Life, Balance is Bullshit. You'll never achieve total and sustainable balance.

Your Bliss Life will forever be in constant flow, and sometimes one Relationship will take precedence over another. Just like Maslow's Hierarchy of Needs, you'll need to set a foundation in your relationships before transcending to the next level.

Your foundation is Self. Self-awareness is the key to unlocking a Bliss Life. Having a strong sense of Self and being able to attune to the needs of Self will set the stage for all your wildest dreams to come true.

If you don't know yourself, your wants, needs, fears, and desires, you'll never know what you truly want. And if you don't know what you want, how can you live a life that fills you with Bliss?

The greatest way to start building a relationship with yourself is to journal. Journaling is one of the most powerful tools we have in creating a Bliss Life.

You can start very simply. Every day write a list of 10 things you like. This is the Wild West of journaling; there are no rules here. Nothing is off-limits. No one has to read this list except you, so don't feel required to list things you think you *should*, but do be specific.

Croissants
Baroque architecture
Matching sweatsuits
Getting likes on selfies on IG
The color purple
Catching people checking out your butt
The Harry Potter book series (not the movies)
Leather boots

See. No rules.

After a few days/weeks of this, you'll see a pattern emerge. If you don't, you can show your list to a trusted friend or family member who won't judge you to help you find the pattern.

This list will give you tremendous insight into your relationship with your Self. Practice self-awareness and take notice of yourself. Do most of your favorite things include being social or anti-social? Your Bliss Life will then have you prioritizing time for more (or less) social activities. Seeing a lot of outdoor adventures on your lists? Time with animals? A need to work towards a higher social purpose, higher paychecks, or both?

When it comes to your Bliss Life, you don't have to sacrifice what you want, but you will have to sacrifice. You CAN have it all. You just can't have it all at the same time.

Remember, Balance is Bullshit.

Once you have gotten into a habit of daily journaling, take it to the next level with journal prompts. There are millions of lists and blog articles, books, and other resources you can use to find some self-discovery prompts.

Here are a few to get you started:

What are some ways I've achieved success?

What gets me excited?

What would be my perfect day?

When do I feel the most proud of myself?

When do I usually give up?

What did my life look like when I was the happiest? How is it now?

What activities drain me?

How can I stretch my comfort zone?

You are looking to build a relationship with Self, so treat yourself like someone you really want to have a relationship with. Get to know your likes and dislikes and spend time treating Self with love, grace, and a little extra attention when you need it.

Get to know who you are and what you truly want. This is the longest and most committed relationship you will ever have, fostering the relationship with Self continuously. This is the first step to creating Bliss Life.

CULTIVATING A RELATIONSHIP WITH A HIGHER POWER

Your relationship with your Higher Power is a personal one. But a belief system is often shared and creates a community — religious leaders or peers who practice a style of worship with you. Spending time connecting with these people helps to strengthen your relationship with your Higher Power, but in the end, it's all about you and the Higher Power you resonate with.

If you are a part of organized religion, there's usually one day or part of one day per week dedicated to community worship.

But committing a few hours per week to your Higher Power relationship and then completely forgetting about it until next week doesn't build a strong relationship. You wouldn't do that with your kids, partner, or boss, so why limit your interaction with your Higher Power?

Integrate your relationship with your Higher Power into your daily life with Study, Meditation, and Prayer.

If you're more on the Spiritual side of things, don't get too hung up on the vernacular. Prayer is, in essence, a moment of gratitude, intention, and reflection — a conversation with your Higher Power.

Your Higher Power is an infinite being with untold knowledge and unlimited love for you. Why would you go through your day, building your Bliss Life, without their insight and guidance? Seems silly when put that way.

I truly believe that the Universe, your Higher Power, and mine, is continuously conspiring to give us every ounce of happiness and everything towards the highest good.

If you are actively reaching and working toward your Bliss Life and it just isn't happening, consider this:

Rejection is redirection — when things don't work out, it's often because our Higher Power has something much **much** better planned for us.

In my own life, I've seen this time after time. I want, wish, and work for something (or someone) so hard, and all I'm met with is rejection. It's only in retrospect that I can see exactly how blessed I am that those paths didn't work out.

Which is why daily relationship-building with your Higher Power is key in co-creating your Bliss Life.

Being attuned to the vibes of your Higher Power, checking in and checking on, can keep you from wasting too much time, energy, and attention on the wrong path for you.

BUILDING YOUR TRIBE - THE INNER CIRCLE

Now that you've built a strong relationship with yo' bad self AND you're working in tandem with your Higher Power towards your Bliss Life, you can find your Tribe.

Your Tribe is the people who fill up your life and help give it more meaning. It is your family, friends, or anyone you choose to surround yourself with. I like to break this down further into your Inner Circle Tribe and your Community Tribe.

Your Inner Circle Tribe is your best people. People who bring out the best in you. You really are the average of the 5 people you hang out with the most.

Take a look at your inner circle. Who do you call/text every day? Who do you spend the most time with? Whose opinions do you value most?

Your Inner Circle Tribe are the relationships you should be the pickiest with. These are people that inspire your greatness. These are the people who celebrate your successes and are also striving for their Bliss Life.

No one's idea of their Bliss Life includes dragging their Inner Circle, kicking, and screaming to success with them. As you grow and develop your relationships and build your Bliss Life, there will be people who don't support you and may even get mad about it.

Most of the time, people who are stuck in lives they'd rather not be living, but are unwilling to take the action and make the changes for themselves, feel personally attacked when you start building your way out of your old life and into your Bliss Life.

Unfortunately, close friends and family can be the first ones to try and talk you out of your goals. No matter the relationship, it's hard to see someone else taking risks and making changes when you're too scared or unwilling to do so. Most people who are stuck in a less than Bliss Life have thoroughly convinced themselves that nothing can be done. They haven't taken hold of the idea that they have the power to make the changes they secretly crave.

When these people see you disproving the rationalizations they have created for themselves, it shakes up their world. They are forced to see you and your power and come face to face with the reality that everything really is your fault (and therefore their fault in their own life). This can cause feelings of anger and resentment.

Do not fear – you are not alone. As you start making different choices, showing up for yourself and others in new and aligned ways, you'll begin to attract people who will support and even help you expand and reach your goals.

Once I started pruning the Negative Nancys in my own life, I saw a radical and explosive transformation in every relationship in my life.

My personal Inner Circle transformation started with a breakup. My partner at the time was a stuck-in-a-rut kind of person — very content with a low vibrational, Non-Bliss Life. So, I sent him packing. It was hard and scary, and there were plenty of "I'm going to die alone" moments.

I started focusing on my relationship with Self. I took myself on dates, went to yoga, and allowed myself to be open to new things.

One day my favorite yoga teacher invited me to a weekend yoga retreat. At the time, I had no money; I was working two jobs and had to get a roommate just to cover rent. But my Higher Power said, "YES." Before I realized what was going on, I was in a car with four other women headed on a four-hour road trip to the retreat.

To say I felt out of place would be an understatement. I felt like the broke, chubby, awkward, unsuccessful one.

But it was all in my head. I hadn't fully released the old version of my self-perception, which was a big part of what was holding me back.

Over that weekend, I formed amazing friendships and was guided to start looking at my life with possibilities. It's not that I hadn't already done a lot in my life. It was that I had plateaued.

This new Inner Circle Tribe gave me insight, guidance, motivation, and belief that I could do, be, and have more.

Within one year, yes 12 short months, I tripled my income, checked off some massive bucket list items, and positioned myself to build a better Bliss Life.

The right Inner Circle reminds you of the power you already have.

Now, your Inner Circle Tribe is more than just good friends; it includes your family as well. Some people have the type of family that gets together for dinner once a week and is constantly involved in each other's lives. This is neither good nor bad; it all depends on the support you receive from them as you start taking steps towards your own Bliss Life.

Your family, and especially your partner, may not be on the same page immediately, and that's okay. You shouldn't expect them to make these monumental changes with you.

As long as they support you, they'll see you becoming happier, and some of those changes will eventually rub off on them, too. Just remember that it's YOUR Bliss Life; you don't have to wait for everyone in your family or your partner to join you before you get started.

STRONG PERSONAL BOUNDARIES - YOUR COMMUNITY TRIBE

Your Community Tribe is the next ring in the circle of people you surround yourself with. This can be family, the ones you don't see as often, and close acquaintances. People in your neighborhood, the PTA, people at church, or your partner's friends and their partners. Your Community Tribe isn't necessarily your Inner Circle of close personal friends but people you engage with regularly.

This, however, does not include co-workers. We'll get to them in the Network relationships.

As you go about creating your Bliss Life, the people who need to be removed, or given limited access to your power, will start to make themselves known.

You're making different choices. You have different priorities, and that's going to trigger some people. You'll hear things like:

"You've changed."
"How long are you going to keep acting like this?"
"Can you just get past this phase already?"
"Who do you think you are?"

Hearing these comments and others like them is particularly hard when they're said by a family member (maybe one you thought you were close to), but remember it's YOUR life, not theirs. You don't have to adopt the values, goals, and lifestyle of people around you just because they have known you for a long time or they believe "that's just not possible for people like us."

Limiting interactions with or even completely cutting people off is hard. We tend to want to do it in a dramatic fashion, letting them know that they are not contributing to our Bliss Life and we're through with them!

The desire to create a dramatic and emotional fight scene stems from a desire to not actually be cut off from them but to shake them into realizing that they are stuck, and we want them to change with us.

I'm sorry to say this well-intentioned attempt at reverse psychology never works.

The best way to limit interactions with someone is simply to stop being available.

Your friend calls for another wild night out, but you're practicing being consistent with your morning and evening routines.

Instead of saying, "Sorry friend, I can't come out. I'm really trying to level up my life, and that means I'm dedicating my time right now to morning and evening routines. You really should try it and stop asking me to go out. Don't you want to support me?"

Which only opens up room for rationalizations and hurt feelings. Instead, try:

"No thanks, have fun!"

Not everyone needs to be privy to the specifics of your Bliss Life efforts, especially if these people will only mock or try to derail you.

Just be unavailable. They'll eventually stop asking, or they'll start to see your changes and ask about what you're doing. Then you can decide how much to share.

IT'S YOUR NETWORK, BABY (AKA YOUR NETWORK IS YOUR NET WORTH)

The next relationship to look at is the one you have with your Network. This relationship includes everyone from your work-bestie, to your boss, to that guy you met at an event last week and should really follow up with.

The relationship you have with your Network is also the relationship you have with your career, not just the people at your job. Be as intentional with the work that you do as you are with the people you do it with.

Treat your career path with care and attention as if it were a person. The work you do for the money you need will have a huge impact on your overall Bliss Life.

The best jobs are ones that pay you to learn new skills that will eventually help you to get an even better job. Even if your J-O-B feels more like a four-letter word, you can still focus on building a better relationship with your Network.

The famous saying by Porter Gale is "Your network is your net worth," meaning your professional

Network dictates how much power and influence you have personally and professionally. The people you know and how much they are invested in you will assist or hinder your effort to rise in the ranks in every conceivable way. This will help you get to where you want to be professionally. No matter what your professional goals are, having a network behind you helps.

Spend conscious energy building better relationships with those you share a workplace with because there's not much worse than waking up to go to a job you hate, with people you hate, every single day.

Set some goals for your Network that include elements of both your career and your colleagues. It can be as simple as "quit the job that is sucking the life force out of me" or more complex like "gain necessary certification and make a career switch."

Both goals involve building relationships with people in the workplace, maybe just not the workplace you're currently in. If you so desire, your Bliss Life will include a job that gives you a sense of freedom, flexibility, and creativity, all while making enough money to live comfortably.

The biggest trick to getting really good at building your Network relationship is to stay curious.

This means taking every opportunity to learn more. Learn more about your craft and your industry. Find ways to sharpen your skills, and most importantly, try to learn everything you can about other people.

Networking events are a little bit nerve-wracking for everyone, even seasoned extraverts. Don't focus on that one person you've got to talk to about the big deal/project/insight/etc.

Instead, focus on building a professional network through giving. Give your undivided attention by offering kudos or helping someone make a really good connection for themselves.

Your job is to be consistent, helpful, and always follow up. Recommend a great local restaurant to a contact and then follow up to see how they liked it. Following up is where most people fail at building a Network.

Focus on the giving — focus on being present and following through with an excellent and organic follow-up. Save sales pitches and other requests for after you've built a relationship. It'll pay dividends.

MONEY, MONEY, MONEY

Money is energy. Once you begin to understand this, your relationship with Money starts to look like your relationship with your Higher Power. No, I'm not suggesting you pray to your money but start looking at it as a co-creator in building your Bliss Life.

Jen Sincero, author of *You Are A Badass At Making Money* and other similar titles, suggests that we take a look at our beliefs surrounding Money by exchanging the word "Money" for the word "Pizza."

This starts to look like:

"Pizza is the root of all evil."
"I'm terrible at managing pizza."
"Pizza changes people."
"It's hard for me to make pizza."
"Wanting pizza makes you a greedy person."
"There's never enough pizza."
"Pizza doesn't grow on trees."

See how silly that sounds? Take the power away from the word money and give it back to yourself.

Start paying attention to your money the same way you'd pay attention to a best friend or a lover.

If you are constantly asking your friend to show up for you, provide the fun, and do everything you ask, and you never give them a second thought after, that friend is going to leave you high and dry one day.

Something that took me way too long to learn is there's a big difference between being able to make money and being able to manage wealth.

Everyone is capable of making money. But some people swear that's just not true; they can't make money to save their lives. Mostly though, they think they can't because they aren't properly motivated.

They say they're broke until the water heater goes out, and, wow, look at that, they came up with eight hundred dollars to fix it.

I like the saying, "You never hear a crackhead say, 'I don't have enough money to smoke today,' don't be out-hustled by a crackhead." While addiction is nothing to joke about, it makes a solid point: Everyone is capable of making money; you just need to find the motivation.

But the *getting* is only half of the relationship.

Some of the best and most common relationship advice is, "Keep dating after you're married."

Meaning don't take your significant other for granted once you've committed to marriage.

The same is true for your relationship with Money. Don't fail the relationship after you've got the money, just because you've "got it."

Pay attention to your money; see where it goes. Show gratitude for the things it brings you.

Have faith that spending money will bring you happiness and that the money will always come back to you.

It reminds me of the song by 38 Special:

"Hold on loosely, but don't let go. If you cling too tightly, you're gonna lose control."

If you don't know where to start building a healthy relationship with money, I suggest taking an inventory of what you do have — a simple list: Incoming and Outgoing.

How much money is coming in? How often? From where? And then keep a record or go back through your bank statements and see where all that money is going. Yet again, knowledge is power. Start building a relationship with money.

HONORING YOUR TIME; IT'S THE MOST VALUABLE THING YOU HAVE

The last step to building your foundation for a Bliss Life is building a better relationship with Time. Have a relationship with and understand where your time goes.

When I think back to my early 20s —no kids, part-time job, unlimited freedom, and limited responsibilities — I wonder, "What did I spend all that time doing?"

The answer is nothing.

I look back at those times and kick myself for not having a better relationship with Time. There's so much I could have accomplished if only I had understood that Time is a finite resource and needs to be treated with respect. *C'est la vie.*

To start building a better relationship with Time, I suggest this exercise:

Make a list of everything you MUST spend time doing. Sleep is at the top of this list. Working for money or caretaking is also usually up there too. Keep these fairly generic for now.

Example list:
Sleep
Work
Commute
Laundry and house cleaning
Grocery shopping and cooking

Next is the fun part. Make a list of the things you WANT to spend time doing. These are the things you've identified that will bring you closer to your Bliss Life.

Example list:
Exercising + Meditating
Self-Care
Reading + Journaling
Date Night
Friend Time
Networking Events
Volunteering

Now, find the time to create a two-week calendar (I do it in Excel because I <3 Excel, but this eventually ends up on my google calendar) with a slot for every hour — from midnight to 11 PM.

Fill in the slots for the MUST DO list first — starting with sleep. I cannot stress this enough. Put sleep first; it will make your life easier, healthier, and happier.

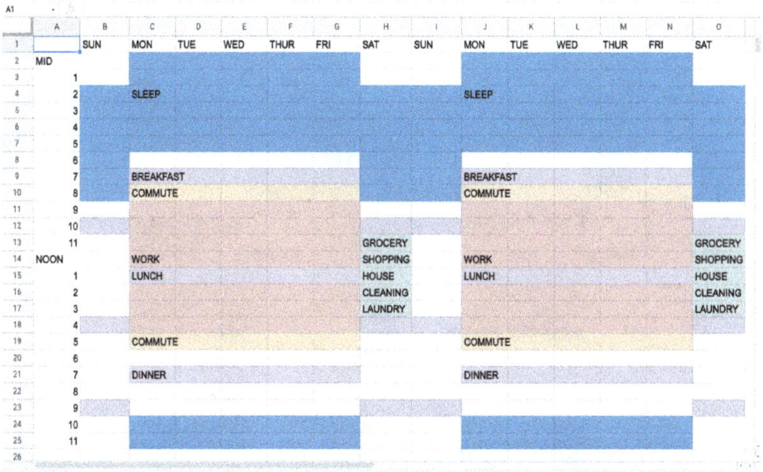
SUN
MON
TUE
WED
THUR
FRI
SAT
SUN
MON
TUE
WED
THUR
FRI
SAT
MID
NOON
SLEEP
SLEEP
BREAKFAST
COMMUTE
BREAKFAST
COMMUTE
GROCERY
SHOPPING
HOUSE
CLEANING
LAUNDRY
WORK
LUNCH
WORK
LUNCH
GROCERY
SHOPPING
HOUSE
CLEANING
LAUNDRY
COMMUTE
COMMUTE
DINNER
DINNER

Now you have a visual representation of your two-week commitments. This, of course, will look different for everyone. And it's not always going to be the same, especially if you don't have a set schedule at your job, if you work nights, if you have two jobs, if you don't commute, etc. Just make sure you get it generally well mapped out.

My two-week commitment looks like this:

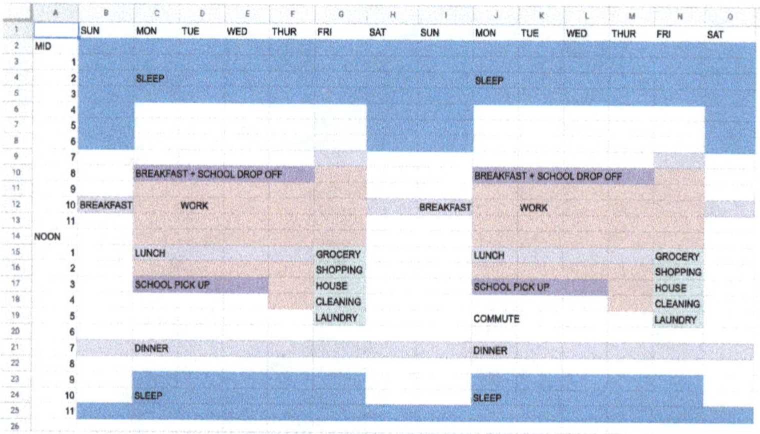

Remember there are 336 hours in two weeks.

7-8 hours of sleep per night is 100 hours of sleep over two weeks of time well spent.

If you work 8 hours a day and we factor in an hour commute each way, that's 100 hours dedicated. 33.6% of your time goes to your Network and Money relationships.

If you've done the math ahead of time, you'll know that means you have roughly 136 hours left in a two-week time period to dedicate to your WANTS.

If we plug in the WANTS from the example list, it will look like this:

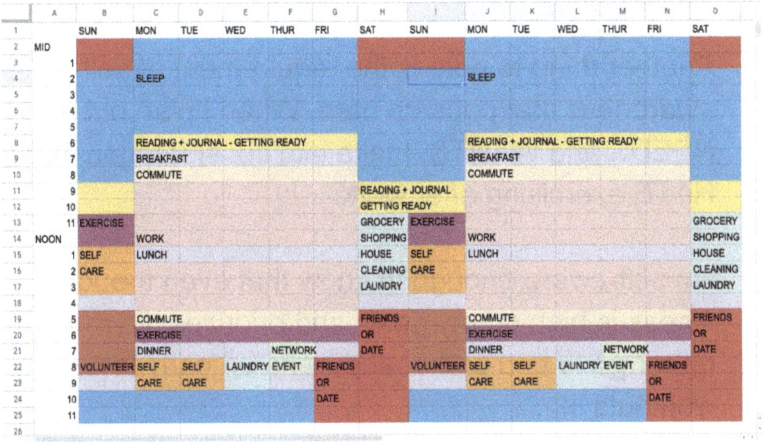

That's 14 hours over two weeks committed to Self-Care, Dates and/or Friends, and Exercise EACH.

My WANTS look like this:

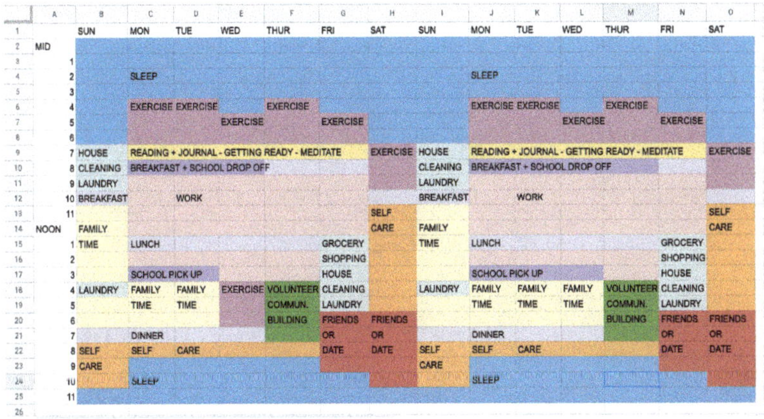

There are a few things to take notice of. My week doesn't stay the same week over week; some things are on a two-week schedule.

Another thing to note is the requirement of self-awareness that pops up here. When I plan out my NEEDS and WANTS, I take into consideration that I HATE exercising after work.

I'm self-aware enough to know that even though fitness is high on my goals and priorities, I'd much rather go to bed earlier and wake up early to get my workouts in.

Remember, it's YOUR Bliss Life. Make it any way you want. Make it magical; you don't owe anyone an explanation.

part 3

EXECUTING ON YOUR GOALS (AKA MAKE THOSE DREAMS COME TRUE)

Executing on your goals is a two-step process.

The planning step and the action step.

Most people are good at either one, but it's the synchronicity of the two that turns goals into reality.

We've covered a lot on the planning step, finding out how you want to feel and visualizing and manifesting what our Bliss Life will look like. We've gotten as far as mapping out the time to dedicate to these new goals.

And yet, we haven't DONE anything. Don't let the planning stage lull you into a false sense of accomplishment. Yes, you've gotten ready, but don't, under any circumstances, stop there.

Work your plan.

Here's where I have an issue with "New Year, New Me." There is nothing wrong with you. You are perfect and whole; you just know that you've got some goals and habits that need an upgrade so you can start living your Bliss Life *as yourself.*

Think about the you five or even ten years ago. You were still you, and as you as you are you today. You've changed, up-leveled, learned, and grown over the years, but you're still YOU.

It's not about a radical 12-week challenge or a total life overhaul. It's about small, simple upgrades to the mindset and choices you make starting today. It's a rearrangement of your priorities today so that future-you can enjoy your Bliss Life sooner and more fully.

After I had my son, I started training for a bodybuilding and fitness competition. I was recently single, struggling with money and self-worth, and focused on attracting a new partner.

I wasn't connected to my Higher Power and spent a lot of time distracting myself from my fears and struggles by going out drinking with low-vibe friends.

I began working closely with a personal trainer, and during our sessions, I'd talk about all the things I was trying to accomplish. Finally, my coach pulled me aside and said, "You CAN have it all, you just can't have it all at the same time."

She explained that high-level fitness competitions took a considerable amount of focus, time, and dedication. She was happy to help me succeed, but it wasn't a realistic goal to have in conjunction with all my other efforts.

So, I quit.

Because, as Seth Godin says in his book *The Dip*, "Winners quit and quitters win."

I assessed my priorities and realized that focusing on my fitness goals wasn't putting me on the path towards my Bliss Life, not at the time anyway.

I spent the next five years working on my Relationships. I made Network moves, I built a better Tribe, and I made peace with my Money. I focused on each Relationship in turn. Because Balance is Bullshit.

I spent one year entirely dedicated to the idea of Wealth, Joy, and Ease. I only focused on the things that would bring me closer to those feelings.

I never said, "Once I get to XYZ place in my life, then I'll go back to fitness competition," because that kind of condition is an impossible place to set oneself.

Instead, I'd say, "Fitness competitions aren't a priority right now." Then I'd see how that felt. And honestly, for five years, I was absolutely content not making weightlifting a priority. Until one day, I wasn't. I found myself in a place where that goal was able to naturally resurface and has again become an active goal.

This is why I don't like setting goals further out than three years. The you three years ago was in a different place, either literally or in your mindset. I like to think of this as Scope. You can only dream and set goals as big as your imagination.

Yes, I can imagine a private jet and a yacht on the French Riviera, but I don't, in my core, believe that those things are a reality for me. (And frankly, I don't even want them right now.)

Manifestation isn't imagining what you want and then wishing it into existence. It's realizing that you attract what you already are.

If you have absolutely no spark of belief that you can own a private jet, then you can never, no not ever, attract that into your life.

But about every three years, if you keep growing and reaching for that next up-level, you'll gain a new Scope, and a new perspective of what you CAN start attracting into your life, and your priorities will change along the way.

Here's an example:

When I was 19, a small-town girl living in a lonely world (no really, I grew up in a very small farm town), I was asked about my career ambitions. I said I wanted to work in fashion. I wanted to work at the most upscale posh designer stores in a fancy big city. I wanted to walk, every morning, into a luxurious storefront in my classic all-black ensemble, latte in hand, and help people pick out the most exquisite products.

So, I did.

There were a few detours and bumps in the road, but by 22, I was working at a high-end retailer in the newest and most fabulous mall, living in a quaint downtown apartment, rocking my all-black-plus-latte look.

Six months later, the sparkle had all but washed off my dream. There was no way I was going to do THIS for the rest of my life.

So almost exactly three years after I'd set that first big, shiny goal, I set another one just as seemingly big and shiny and only just barely out of reach.

And then, three years after that, another goal, and another...

I doubled my income every three years since the age of 19, and if you look back to the job you had at 19, you probably have too.

There's no reason you can't do it again, and again, and again.

Now I breeze into stores I'd dreamt about working in and buy MYSELF those exquisite products, as long as they fit within my Money Relationship.

What I'm saying is that you don't have to dream big, and you don't have to bust your ass for 30, 40, or 50 years to hopefully get to the dream you set at 19.

Success begets motivation. When you start seeing yourself, through small changes, make milestone achievements, THAT will fuel you through to the next success. And when you keep that momentum going, there's nothing out of reach for your Bliss Life.

Maybe I should start looking at Airbnb's in the south of France...

KICKING ASS AND TAKING NAMES

Here are two quotes from very smart men:

"I'm not a businessman, I'm a Business, man" – Jay-Z

"You can do anything for three months" - Richard Bliss

Ah yes, Mr. Beyonce and my dad. Two smart guys with quotes that go together better than I'm sure either of them realizes.

Just like a business, you can look at yourself, your time, and your goals in quarters because you really can do anything for three months.

Throughout this process, you have probably composed a lengthy list of goals in each of the 6 Relationships, and now you know that trying to do them all at once is a really terrible idea. YOU WILL BURN OUT.

Look at your life as if you were a business. What are the top priorities for the year? How do you want to feel at the end of it?

So, you want to be Successful? Great, same.

But how are you defining “success?”

Is it money in the bank? A new Birkin? A specific number of followers on Instagram?

There’s no judgment here – it’s your life and your definition of success.

So, now you’ve clearly defined your success measure, what are you going to do about it? Change jobs, pick up a side hustle, save spare change until you can buy that status symbol item, take a course on how to get more Instagram followers??

How are you going to track your progress?

Stop. This one is important.

Remember the momentum I told you about? This is where you find it. Whatever your goal is, you have got to make it trackable — figure out a way to see your progress over time.

In fitness, they refer to these types of trackable goals as a “non-scale victory,” something related to the goal that’s not specifically tied to the progress of the goal.

For example, if your goal to feel more successful means you want to get a promotion and a raise, figure out a way to track your progress besides actually getting the promotion.

Try a spreadsheet (see, I really do love them), or use a paper or digital calendar to track the daily progress you've made. Set milestones — mini-goals to help fuel your progress.

Did a killer job on a project? Write it down; make it a milestone.

Told a buddy "no" when invited to take off work early and meet them for an extra early happy hour with the new cute bartender? Write it down.

Remember you're committed for three months. You're not saying goodbye to a social life forever; you're just focusing on this particular goal right now.

When your eye is on the prize, or goal, it's easier to start identifying things that will either lead you closer to that goal or detract from it.

Saying "yes" to the right opportunities and "no" to the wrong ones becomes crystal clear.

After three months, apply for the promotion, sit your boss down and present all the milestones you've created over the course of your effort and sell yourself.

One of two things will happen. You'll either get the promotion, or you won't.

I'm not going to tell you to "keep a positive attitude" if you don't get the promotion. No, I encourage you to get curious. It's not an L for loss; it's an L for lessons.

Did your boss provide you with significant feedback that will help you reach your goals in the next three months?

Is this rejection just redirection and a chance for you to apply for a position at a different company with a title change and pay increase? Stay curious, but don't give up.

REMOVING YOUR FRICTION POINTS

Your Bliss Life is yours for the taking. It'll take subtle shifts in your self-identity, your mindset, your Relationships, and your focus.

Setting and achieving your goals is all about the small steps you take to get there.
Do common things with uncommon consistency.

Sometimes we fail. Sometimes we quit. Even though we really didn't want to; it just got too hard.

Surprise! Life is hard.

But you don't have to make it harder on yourself. Reaching your goals and achieving your Bliss Life is possible, and it all comes down to the tiniest of details.

I wake up every morning at 4 AM to write in my journal and then workout for two hours with a personal trainer. That's hard. I don't always want to do it at that moment. I know I want to achieve my fitness goals, and I know that the best way to do so is to wake up at 4 am. But there's a moment, a window of time, where I rationalize to myself why I don't actually REALLY want or need to go.

I tell myself I can quit my goal, just for one day. I mean, it's fine, what's one day going to do in the long run?

I could choke to death on the excuses. It's a hard moment. But there are a few things I can do to make it just the tiniest fraction less hard — setting out my gym clothes the night before, for example.

Even I roll my eyes at this. Yes, so simple-minded, so obvious, so overdone. But having my gym clothes next to my phone, across my room, makes me get up, walk over, and then...

Whoosh! It's magic. It's too easy; it's SO easy to grab my gym clothes and go change.

I also set my coffee maker for 4 am because it's one less Friction Point.

Friction Points are the moments we're posed with an option, a time to make a choice. The more Friction Points between where you are and where you want to be to reach your goal, the less likely you are to get there.

The true secret to reaching any goal is to identify the Friction Points along the way and combat them ahead of time.

That friend calling you for a three-margarita lunch and binge-watching The Bachelorette, it's not a Friction Point. No, it's not a decision if your phone is on airplane mode during your focus work hours.

Eliminate the opportunity to make the wrong decision because we're human and self-control is a muscle. The more you work it during the day, the more feeble it becomes.

This is why most choices that aren't in alignment with our goals are made at night or when we're stressed and overwhelmed.

Grace Is More Than a Blessing

We end with Grace.

We are all guilty of needing a little more Grace in our lives, especially for ourselves. You will not be perfect. Your Bliss Life will not be perfect, so don't expect perfection.

You are just as worthy today as you were yesterday, and as you will be tomorrow.

Don't let one or three or thirty slip-ups bring you down.

Remember, “winners quit and quitters win.” Stay curious about yourself, your Relationships, your Goals, and your Friction Points.

Pivot when necessary. Start to identify when to stick it out and when you’re just spinning your wheels.

Keep your goals:

> Emotional — How you want to feel.
>
> Personal — Who you want to be.
>
> Literal — What you’re specifically going to do.
>
> Measurable — How you track your progress.
>
> Sustainable — Something that will stay with you long-term.

You can do anything for three months, cause you’re a Business, man.

Nothing bad ever happens when we set and hold strong boundaries, with and for ourselves.

Acknowledgements

The lines of co-workers, friends, and family becomes blurred with BlissPoint. This book was such a pleasure to write, I'm grateful for BlissPoint and the support they showed me through the entire process.

Gratitude to be expressed to my Tribe and Network:

Richard and Stephanie, thank you for the access, opportunity and faith that continues to push me further in my career and my Bliss Life.

Marshall, my best boy who shows me how to be curious and kind every single day.

Marcie, Claire, Sheena, Kimberly, and Kiera, my boss babe dream team, I couldn't do half of what I do without your unique support, insight and love.

Lisa, and Alicia, my inner circle, without you I never could have seen what I can become. Both of you inspire me daily.

About the Author

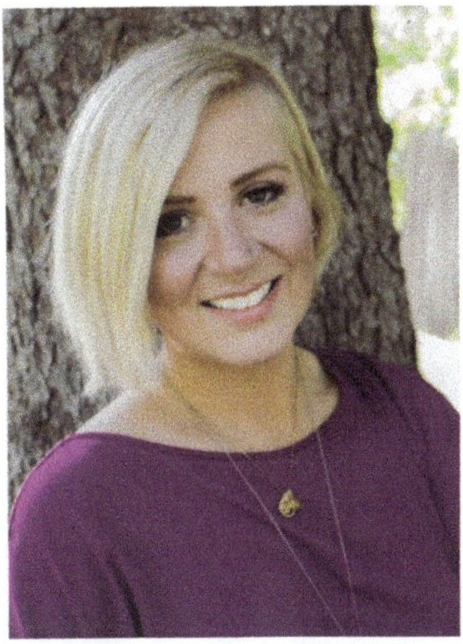

Lia Bliss is the Director of Strategy and Sales Enablement and Lead LinkedIn Trainer at BlissPoint Consulting. In the ever-changing economic and social media driven world, Lia enables sales leaders and their teams to become masters of their online presence and mindset. She is an engaging speaker with deep subject expertise in LinkedIn algorithms, social selling, and the day-to-day habits it takes to build engagement. Lia is also a mindset coach whose mission is to empower others to live their best "Bliss Life."

Follow Lia on:
LinkedIn - linkedin.com/in/liabliss
Instagram - @bestliabliss

www.ingramcontent.com/pod-product-compliance
Lightning Source LLC
Chambersburg PA
CBHW060751100426
42813CB00004B/769
* 9 7 8 1 7 3 6 8 4 6 2 9 2 *